BUREAU OF LAND MANAGEMENT- California

National Conservation Lands

Five-Year Strategy: 2013–2018

I0448562

BLM

California

NATIONAL
CONSERVATION
LANDS

Fort Ord National Monument

California Coastal National Monument

INTRODUCTION:

In 2000, under the Clinton Administration, a new national land conservation system was created by order of the Secretary of the Interior, and the Bureau of Land Management (BLM) was given the honor of managing this new system of public lands. Codified into Federal law in the 2009 Omnibus Public Land Management Act enacted by President Barack Obama, it is officially called the National Landscape Conservation System and includes a wide range of special areas, called National Conservation Lands, on the BLM administered public lands throughout the country, mostly in the West.

Nationally, the BLM manages more than 880 units of the System and approximately 27 million acres including national monuments, national conservation areas, national scenic and historic trails, wild and scenic rivers, wilderness areas, wilderness study areas, and other special areas designated by Congress and the President. These areas are characteristic of the diversity of the West itself—from red-rock deserts and rugged ocean coastlines, to deep river canyons and broad Alaskan tundra. Many areas are remote and wild but others are surprisingly accessible. The mission of the National Landscape Conservation System is to conserve, protect, and restore these nationally significant landscapes that are recognized for their outstanding cultural, ecological, and scientific values.

To begin to mold a vision for how to care for these lands in the long-term, the BLM developed The National Landscape Conservation System 15-Year Strategy 2010–2025. This document can be viewed on the BLM website at: www.blm.gov/wo/st/en/info/newsroom/2011/september/NR_09_30_2011.html

The document that follows is BLM-California's detailed five-year strategy for implementing this vision on the 171 units of National Conservation Lands covering five million acres under BLM-California's jurisdiction. These National Conservation Lands include many of the most spectacular areas in the State, from snow-crested mountains to the rugged Pacific Coast and through the Great Central Valley to the starkly beautiful California Desert.

This BLM-California strategy is designed to provide a starting point for discussions with partners, stakeholders, and members of the public to get their views on what's needed to ensure wise management of these public resources, and what role and actions they can take to support and contribute to the management of these special places.

Some actions discussed here are intended to implement BLM-wide actions listed in the national strategy. Others are California-specific, but based on the national framework.

Santa Rosa and San Jacinto Mountains
National Monument

This document is designed to guide the thought processes, and, hopefully, inform the decisions that BLM-California is entrusted to make.

It is important to acknowledge the context and limitations of this California-focused strategy. Implementation is contingent on available budget and staffing, as well as consistency with law, policy, and approved decisions. The strategy does not amend BLM land use plans or replace local planning or decision-making processes. Instead, it is a "living" document that will be regularly updated as successes are achieved, priorities updated, and opportunities arise.

This strategy describes what BLM-California aspires to do over the next five years to implement the National Conservation Lands strategy, consistent with national and BLM-California priorities. A few of these actions will begin in 2013, with others beginning as late as 2018.

Some of these actions may be accomplished by the State Office, while others may be accomplished by respective BLM District or Field Offices with the help of local partners and volunteers. Not all actions will apply to every Field Office, land designation type, or acre of public land. Options for locally unique adaptations of State and National-level strategic goals and priorities are encouraged, where appropriate.

Hopefully, this strategy will inform readers as to how BLM-California plans to achieve its legally mandated mission to conserve, protect, and restore these nationally significant lands in BLM's care. BLM-California invites all those who care about these special areas, including stakeholders, partners, friends groups, volunteers, and communities to join with us in identifying and achieving common goals for the benefit of current and future generations.

For additional information on this strategy, contact BLM-California National Conservation Lands co-leads Mark Conley (916) 978-4641 mconley@blm.gov or Bob Wick (916) 978-4665 rwick@blm.gov.

Headwaters Forest Reserve

North Fork American Wild and Scenic River

Table 1: Components of the National Conservation Lands in California

- **National Monuments**: California Coastal, Carrizo Plain, Fort Ord, Santa Rosa and San Jacinto Mountains

- **National Conservation Area**: King Range

- **Forest Reserve**: Headwaters

- **Outstanding Natural Area**: Piedras Blancas Light Station

- **Wild and Scenic Rivers**: Amargosa, North Fork American, Cottonwood Creek, Eel, Klamath, Merced, Trinity, Tuolumne

- **National Historic and Scenic Trails**: California, Juan Bautista de Anza, Old Spanish, Pacific Crest

- **Wilderness Areas**: 85 Wilderness Areas

- **Wilderness Study Areas**: 67 Wilderness Study Areas

Figure 1: Locations of the National Conservation Lands in California

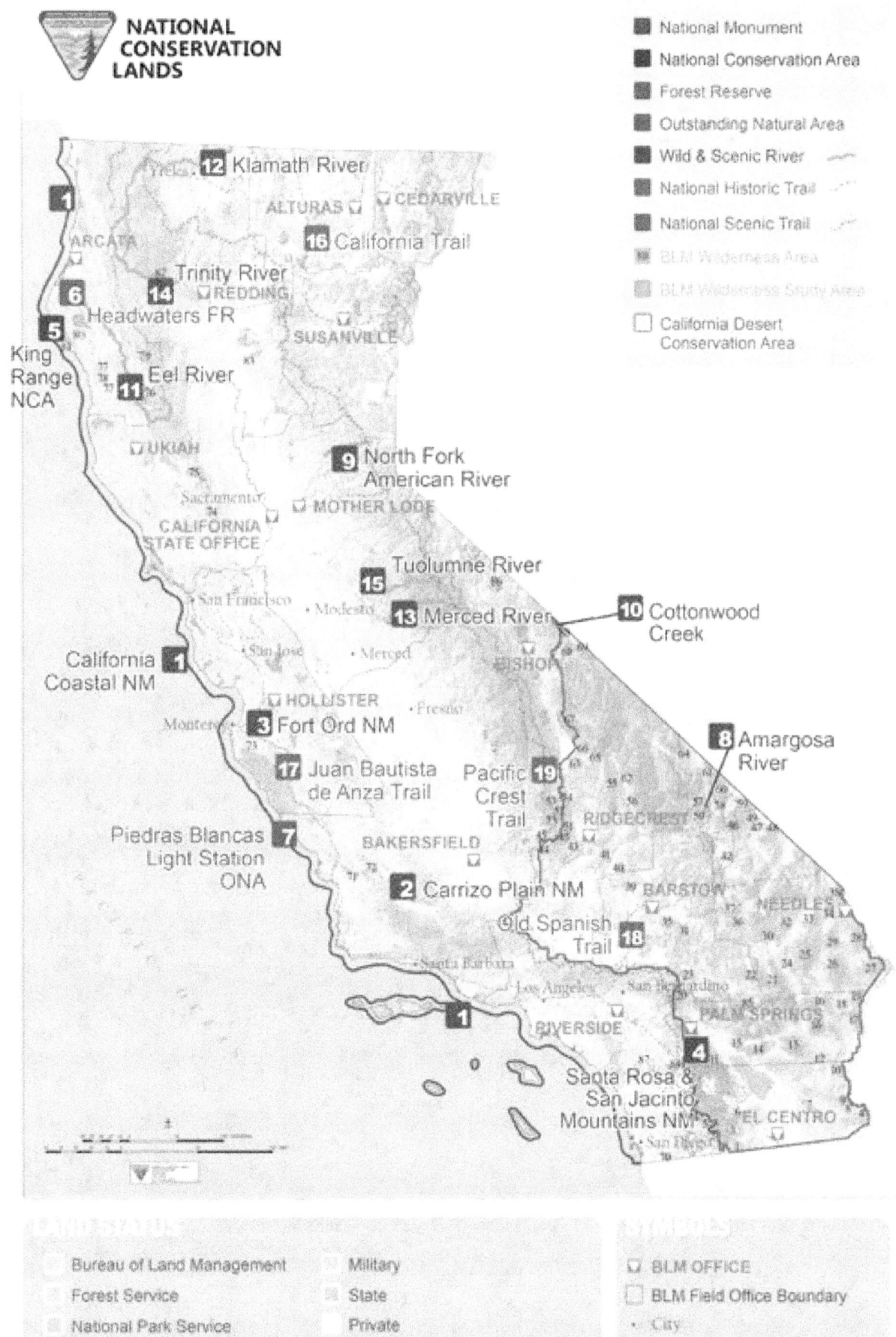

NATIONAL CONSERVATION LANDS

National Monument
National Conservation Area
Forest Reserve
Outstanding Natural Area
Wild & Scenic River
National Historic Trail
National Scenic Trail
BLM Wilderness Area
BLM Wilderness Study Area
California Desert Conservation Area

12 Klamath River
15 California Trail
14 Trinity River
Headwaters FR
6
5
King Range NCA
11 Eel River
9 North Fork American River
Tuolumne River
15
13 Merced River
10 Cottonwood Creek
California Coastal NM **1**
3 Fort Ord NM
17 Juan Bautista de Anza Trail
Pacific Crest Trail
19
8 Amargosa River
Piedras Blancas Light Station ONA **7**
2 Carrizo Plain NM
Old Spanish Trail
18
1
4
Santa Rosa & San Jacinto Mountains NM

Bureau of Land Management
Forest Service
National Park Service
Fish and Wildlife Service
Military
State
Private
Reservations and Rancherias

BLM OFFICE
BLM Field Office Boundary
City

BLM California
National Conservation Lands

5-Year Strategy

Conservation

Conserve,
Protect, Restore

Living Laboratories
Citizen Science
Science Team / Symposium
State Director Grants
Priority Acquisitions
Landscape Level Approach
Restoring Natural Processes

Community

Heritage

Partnering
for Stewardship

Citizen Integration
Gateway Communities
Service First
Friends Groups
Social Media Networks
Eco/Geotourism
Resource Advisory Councils

Connecting
Youth

Educate, Engage, Employ
Youth Summit Implementation
Field School
Youth Resource Monitoring
& Restoration
Environmental Education
Outdoors Cool
Place-Based Curriculum

Communicate the Conservation & Heritage Identity
Messaging and Identity Continuity—Signing, Web Design, Social Media, etc.
Sound Business Practices—Transparency & Accountability

BLM California
National Conservation Lands

Top Priority Strategic Actions

Conservation

- **Inventory:** Conduct inventories of the conservation values for which areas were designated.

- **Protect:** Use conservation values inventories and science (including citizen science) to enhance knowledge of conditions and trends affecting conservation values in designated areas, and where appropriate to design management measures to protect or enhance values over time.

- **Manage Use:** Evaluate proposed uses and use levels of the National Conservation Lands to determine compatibility and ensure consistency with protection of conservation values, limiting or prohibiting uses that are incompatible.

Heritage

- **Educate youth:** Use the National Conservation Lands as living classrooms to promote environmental literacy.

- **Engage youth:** Provide opportunities to youth, especially diverse and under-served youth, to perform on-the-ground work to build a connection to the land.

- **Employ youth:** Provide training and career pathways through youth organizations, internships, and direct hiring.

Community

- **Gateway Communities:** Establish and support partnerships with Gateway Communities in all Field Offices.

- **Partnered Delivery Across Boundaries:** Establish, support, and strengthen partnerships with other federal and state agencies, tribes, and state and local governments.

- **Tourism and Economies:** Support and showcase amenity-based, quality-of-life values that have benefits to both visitors and local community members and economies.

North Algodones Dunes Wilderness

NATIONAL CONSERVATION LANDS STRATEGY

BLM-California advances the four main themes and priority goals developed for the national strategy. For each theme, BLM-California has included a short statement identifying the state's strategic approach. To implement goals under each theme, BLM-California has identified various action items for completion over the next five years. The highest priority action items are indicated with a red rectangle. Additional detailed tasks and implementing actions will be developed during implementation.

Theme 1: Ensuring the Conservation, Protection, and Restoration of National Conservation Lands Values. Enact conservation measures within the National Conservation Lands, use science to further conservation, and provide uses compatible with National Conservation Land resources and values.

Theme 2: Collaboratively Managing the National Conservation Lands as Part of the Larger Landscape. Practice better conservation through collaborative management.

Theme 3: Raising Awareness of the Value and Benefits of the BLM's National Conservation Lands. Raise public awareness and understanding of the National Conservation Lands, cultivate relationships, promote community stewardship of BLM-managed public land, and provide for use and enjoyment of present and future generations.

Theme 4: Building upon BLM's Commitment to Conservation. Promote a model of conservation excellence internally, through improved understanding and fully integrating the National Conservation Lands within the BLM.

Owens Peak Wilderness

Theme 1: Ensuring the Conservation, Protection, and Restoration of National Conservation Lands Values

State Strategic Approach: Maintain and improve the character and over-all natural ecosystem function of each National Conservation Land unit in this dynamic time of global climate change and societal challenges.

Goal 1A: Clearly communicate that the conservation, protection, and restoration of National Conservation Lands' values are the highest priority in the planning and management of the National Conservation Lands consistent with the designating legislation or Presidential proclamation.

State Level Actions:

1. Conduct trainings and webinars to assist District and Field Offices with implementing the new National Conservation Lands manuals. ▪

2. Ensure that new, revised, and amended Resource Management Plans protect values of National Conservation Lands. ▪

3. Evaluate at least two Resource Management Plans annually to assess progress in implementing protection of values of National Conservation Lands. ▪

4. Train a cadre of all-hazard resource advisors to understand National Conservation Lands values and policies so that at least one advisor is present at hazardous events, such as fires or oil spills, at an affected National Conservation Lands unit. ▪

5. Establish conservation and restoration priorities for wilderness, wilderness study areas, scenic and historic trails, wild and scenic rivers, and other National Conservation Land units without specific planning.

6. Establish a process and criteria for the State Director to award funding to strategic National Conservation Lands projects.

7. Engage statewide stakeholders for input on management of National Conservation Lands in California, including implementation of this strategy. Include the U. S. Forest Service, the National Park Service, the Fish and Wildlife Service, the California Department of Fish and Wildlife, the California State Parks and other partners in stewardship.

Conservation Lands Foundation

The Conservation Lands Foundation is the only non-governmental organization dedicated solely to conserving, protecting, and restoring the National Conservation Lands in partnership with BLM. The Foundation has worked to ensure that the friends groups that support the National Conservation Lands have the financial and strategic support to be successful. There are now close to 50 groups in the Friends Grassroots Network. The Foundation is working to launch a new restoration program and plan to provide new funding for conservation projects in 2013 to support on-the-ground projects that improve wildlife habitat and support the preservation of cultural resources on the National Conservation Lands. Since its founding in 2007, the organization has granted over two million dollars to organizations in California and around the West.

King Range National Conservation Area

Goal 1B: Expand understanding of the National Conservation Lands values through assessment, inventory, and monitoring.

State Level Actions:

1. Continue baseline inventories of natural and cultural resources on National Conservation Lands. ▪

    a. Complete trail condition assessments and inventories of national scenic and historic trails.

    b. Inventory the resources, objects, and values for which national monuments, national conservation areas, and similar designations were established.

    c. Compare current wilderness study area conditions to originally inventoried conditions to determine restoration priorities.

2. Design data collection protocols to monitor resources and management practices that are consistent, repeatable, and reliable, in concert with partners, to ensure that information applies to landscapes across jurisdictional boundaries.

    a. Establish a statewide interdisciplinary team to improve consistency of monitoring protocols for wild and scenic rivers and national scenic and historic trails.

3. Collaborate with other federal, state, and local agencies as well as the public to implement the BLM's Assessment, Inventory, and Monitoring (AIM) strategy.

    a. Work with the Washington Office and the National Operations Center to incorporate the AIM strategy into wilderness character monitoring.

4. Develop new and expand existing agreements to facilitate inventory and monitoring with organizations such as the Great Basin Institute, the Chicago Botanical Garden, the American Conservation Experience, the Student Conservation Association, and other non-governmental organizations.

5. Develop citizen science partnerships to involve California's young people and local residents in National Conservation Lands gateway communities.

6. Develop an interactive website and use social media to facilitate citizen reporting monitoring data, resource impacts, and conditions of resources.

7. Develop a wilderness study area monitoring strategy.

Goal 1C: Provide a scientific foundation for decision-making.

State Level Actions:

1. Establish a science team consisting of BLM staff, university researchers, and other scientists to develop a California science strategy that includes assessments of ecosystem vulnerabilities and research needs.

   a. Complete inventories of National Conservation Lands natural and cultural resources. ▪

   b. Prioritize applied research for basing mitigation and adaptation actions under changing climate conditions and monitoring that determines effectiveness of management actions. ▪

   c. Support data needs for ecosystem-process models used to forecast environmental changes. ▪

   d. Collaborate with National Conservation Land units from the same ecoregion in adjacent states and with similarly protected areas in Baja California and Sonora, Mexico to enhance understanding of ecological and sociological processes of National Conservation Lands in each California ecoregion of California.

2. Make research results readily available to BLM staff, partners, and the public.

   a. Distribute significant research findings that meet the Department of the Interior's and the BLM's science standards through state and unit webpages.

3. Strengthen and expand existing partnerships with U.S. Geological Survey, Natural Resource Conservation Service, U.S. Forest Service Research Stations, Landscape Conservation Collaboratives, Cooperative Ecosystem Study Units, Joint Ventures, and others.

4. Expand opportunities for volunteers and youth corps teams to work with scientists conducting research and monitoring on National Conservation Lands.

Goal 1D: Use the National Conservation Lands as an outdoor laboratory and demonstration center for new and innovative management that aids in the conservation, protection, and restoration of National Conservation Land areas.

State Level Actions:

1. Encourage citizen participation and delivery of education and interpretation programs on National Conservation Lands. Build on

Carrizo Plain National Monument
Science Partnership

The Carrizo Plain National Monument is managed by BLM in partnership with The Nature Conservancy and the California Department of Fish and Wildlife. It spans 246,000 acres and provides refuge for multiple endangered animal and plant species. The Carrizo Plain is the largest remaining remnant of the original San Joaquin Valley habitat, and consequently is of prime historic and scientific interest. A long-term study of the ecological impacts of introduced European grasses, begun several years ago under a cooperative agreement with the University of California, Berkeley, has already provided valuable information about the giant kangaroo rat and other endangered species and informed management decisions regarding ways to improve and maintain kangaroo rat habitat. The Plains' preservation is vital to the survival of the habitat and wildlife it supports.

Carrizo Plain National Monument

existing programs such as National Public Lands Day, National Trails Day, National Science Week, and other events. ▪

2. Strengthen and expand partnerships to reach diverse and economically disadvantaged young people through cooperative agreements with youth organizations like the California Conservation Corps, the Los Angeles Conservation Corps, the Student Conservation Corps, the American Conservation Experience, the Great Basin Institute, and AmeriCorps to provide important field work on National Conservation Lands. ▪

3. Promote the National Conservation Lands to universities and research institutions.

   a. Host statewide National Conservation Lands Science Symposia with educational institutions, other government agencies, non-profit organizations, and non-governmental organizations.

4. Promote and pursue innovative techniques for restoring ecological processes and adapt successfully applied techniques among National Conservation Lands units as appropriate.

5. Share research findings in the BLM daily report, Newsbytes, and other media outlets.

6. Work with academic institutions and youth organizations to implement field school programs and other research and education opportunities to meet science needs.

Goal 1E: Limit discretionary uses to those compatible with the conservation, protection, and restoration of the values for which National Conservation Lands were designated.

State Level Actions:

1. Evaluate Resource Management Plans and analyze discretionary uses for impacts on National Conservation Land values. Ensure that discretionary uses identified for National Conservation Lands in the California Desert are compatible with their administration for conservation purposes. ▪

2. Advise National Conservation Lands program managers when proposed projects may be incompatible with values of the National Conservation Lands.

   a. Develop notification criteria and triggers, similar to those in the Rights-of-Way section of BLM Manual *National Monuments,*

National Conservation Areas, and Similar Designations (MS-6220). ▪

3. Develop protocols to monitor values of National Conservation Lands. ▪

4. Manage National Conservation Lands adaptively in a timely manner. ▪

5. Use National Conservation Lands as priority mitigation areas to off-set resource losses on other public lands provided that the proposed mitigation is appropriate to environmental conditions of the lands and contributes to values of the National Conservation Lands.

Goal 1F: Manage facilities in a manner that conserves, protects, and restores National Conservation Lands values.

State Level Actions:

1. Design and build facilities that enhance or harmonize natural and cultural resources of each National Conservation Lands unit using the BLM's *Guidelines for a Quality Built Environment.*

    a. Use "green" products for all building facilities for maintenance, construction, etc. to reflect conservation and sustainability values.

    b. Build facilities that qualify for LEED certification.

2. Incorporate Landscape Architect and Landscape Ecologist skills and functions into appropriate positions in the California Table of Organization to participate in the design of BLM facilities and mitigations on a National Conservation Lands unit. Consult with landscape architects in the design of BLM facilities so that they function to conserve energy resources, qualify for LEED certification, and sustain the conservation values of surrounding ecosystems. Involve a landscape ecologist to provide design and oversight for mitigation of large-scale renewable energy projects in the California Desert.

3. Site visitor centers and administrative facilities developed for National Conservation Lands in local communities.

Shoshone Gateway Community

Amargosa Wild and Scenic River

The small community of Shoshone is internationally recognized as an "ecosystem destination" thanks to the rich natural and cultural resources of the Amargosa River and the dedication and foresight of community leaders, including the proprietor of the Shoshone Inn. The Amargosa River, designated by Congress as a Wild and Scenic River, is an internationally known birding site: 259 bird species have been documented in this desert oasis. A naturalist from the PRBO Conservation Science leads guided hikes and tours for visitors. The nearby China Ranch Date Farm is rich in history: the Old Spanish National Historic Trail crosses the area, along with remnants of the historic Tonopah and Tidewater Railroad. With major support from the Amargosa Conservancy, community leaders and volunteers have provided hundreds of hours of support to BLM by informing and educating visitors about the Amargosa region and gathering essential data to gain a clearer understanding of the water resources of the Amargosa Basin.

Tunnison Mountain Wilderness Study Area

Theme 2: Collaboratively Managing National Conservation Lands as Part of the Larger Landscape

State Strategic Approach: National Conservation Lands in California are part of larger ecosystems and ecoregions. Partnerships with local communities and other land management agencies can ensure an ecosystem- or ecoregion-based approach to planning and managing lands effectively and sustainably.

Goal 2A: Emphasize an ecosystem-based approach to manage the National Conservation Lands in the context of the surrounding landscape.

State Level Actions:

1. Manage cultural landscapes in partnership with tribes, state agencies, and private landowners for the greatest conservation benefit. ▪

2. Ensure that environmental analysis of renewable energy and other projects consider mitigation and compensation for impacted values to National Conservation Lands. ▪

3. Develop criteria for identifying mitigation and compensation for impacts to National Conservation Land values (e. g. visual, recreation, etc.) that currently have no criteria in place. ▪

4. Implement large-scale ecological corridors within landscapes.

    a. Identify and designate, as a component of the National Conservation Lands, the BLM-administered public lands in the California Desert Conservation Area managed for conservation purposes, pursuant to the *Omnibus Public Land Management Act of 2009* (P.L. 111-11). ▪

    b. Link the California Coastal National Monument, BLM coastal properties, and other coastal conservation lands by working collaboratively with the California Department of Fish and Wildlife, California State Parks and Recreation, the California Coastal Conservancy, the California Coastal Commission, and other agencies. ▪

5. Mitigate for project impacts occurring on public lands through restoration and acquisition of inholdings within National Conservation Lands.

a. Develop mitigation criteria and priorities for acquisition of inholdings within National Conservation Lands.

b. Develop mitigations and compensation standards and ratios for impacts to National Conservation Land values. Use a wildlife mitigation protocol as a model for other resource values. (e.g., 5 to 1 acres for wildlife) for National Conservation Lands.

6. Utilize existing large-scale assessments such as Rapid Ecoregional Assessments, wildlife corridor mapping, cultural resource inventories, and wilderness characteristic inventories to inform regional collaborative planning and effective land acquisition.

7. Initiate and participate in vulnerability assessments for critical resources at risk from direct and indirect impacts of climate change.

Goal 2B: Adopt a cross-jurisdictional, community-based approach to landscape-level conservation planning and management.

State Level Actions:

1. Develop and maintain cooperative agreements with gateway communities, stewardship groups, educational institutions, and friends groups to accomplish priority on-the-ground work, and address key issues such as biodiversity, connectivity, and climate change. ▪

a. Expand Service First Agreements and strengthen co-management across landscapes such as those already in effect for the California Coastal National Monument, the Santa Rosa and San Jacinto Mountains National Monument, the Inyo Mountains Wilderness, and other co-managed National Conservation Lands. ▪

b. Enhance communication among BLM National Conservation Lands staff, non-governmental organizations, partners, and the public to achieve common goals.

2. Engage Tribes: ▪

a. Develop agreements with tribes to identify and protect lands that are critical to the long-term ecosystem functions of the landscape. ▪

b. Identify and protect culturally significant features on National Conservation Lands.

c. Coordinate with tribes to facilitate traditional tribal uses on National Conservation Lands.

Pacific Crest Trail Association

The Pacific Crest National Scenic Trail (PCNST) zigzags 2,650 miles across three states from Mexico to Canada, including 220 scenic miles managed by BLM in California. With many land owners involved, the Pacific Crest Trail Association (PCTA) performs a critical role in managing and coordinating efforts to protect, preserve, and promote the trail's world-class significance for the enjoyment of hikers and equestrians and for the value that scenic wildlands provide to all people. In partnership with BLM, U.S. Forest Service, National Park Service, California State Parks, local agencies, and other stakeholders, the PCTA delivers high-quality trail construction and maintenance, restoration, and other trail and land management activities along the trail. In 2012, the PCTA cadre of volunteers contributed more than 115,000 hours and over $1.2 million to maintain and protect the PCNST in California, Oregon, and Washington.

Sacatar Trail Wilderness

3. Acquire inholdings within National Conservation Lands unit boundaries from willing sellers.

    a. Contact inholders at least once every five years to determine their interest in selling private land or establishing conservation easements.

    b. Develop supplemental California-specific criteria to establish acquisition and easement priorities.

    c. Pursue funding for acquisitions within priority components of the National Conservation Lands such as National Monuments, National Conservation Areas, Wilderness, Wild and Scenic Rivers, and National Historic and Scenic Trails.

    d. Coordinate with state agencies, non-profit organizations, and other partners for successful BLM-California National Conservation Lands acquisitions.

Goal 2C: Work with Congress, tribes, other federal and state agencies, and national and local communities to identify and protect lands that are critical to the long-term ecological sustainability of the landscape.

Action Combined with Goals 2A and 2B.

Goal 2D: Adopt a community-based approach to recreation and visitor services delivery consistent with the conservation purpose of the National Conservation Lands and the socio-economic goals of the local community.

State Level Actions:

1. Develop new agreements and maintain existing partnerships with gateway communities to support outdoor recreation opportunities. ▪

2. Develop new and expand existing cooperative agreements with partners for increasing involvement of young people in managing recreation and visitor services on National Conservation Lands. ▪

3. Build community-based recreation and visitor services programs that emphasize sustainable tourism for National Conservation Lands.

    a. Collaborate with the California Roundtable on Recreation, Parks, and Tourism to connect statewide recreation lands with the National Conservation Lands.

b. Implement recommendations from the President's multi-agency tourism initiative to increase travel and international visitors to the National Conservation Lands.

c. Provide accurate, timely, consistent information to local governments, tourism providers, and chambers of commerce.

4. Conduct economic benefit analyses of recreation and tourism options in key gateway communities where studies do not currently exist.

5. Conduct visitor use surveys, with Office of Management and Budget approval, on targeted National Conservation Lands.

Humboldt County Backyard's
Outdoors Cool Program

As part of the America's Great Outdoors initiative aimed at getting young people outdoors more often, the BLM-Arcata Field Office has been coordinating with multiple partners to produce public service announcements (PSAs) with the slogan "Outdoors Cool!" Each PSA delivers a dual message about the importance of experiencing nature firsthand and the locations of natural areas in Humboldt County, such as the Headwaters Forest Reserve and Trinidad Gateway to the California Coastal National Monument. A new version, called "Indoors Not" depicts young people inside playing video games, watching DVDs, texting friends, and being bombarded by sounds until they are overwhelmed. A door opens and they are invited to come outside and explore an ancient redwood forest with friends. These PSAs, which have aired in movie theaters and other venues, are proving to be excellent communication tools to get kids outdoors.

Amargosa Wild and Scenic River

Theme 3: Raising Awareness of the Benefits of BLM National Conservation Lands

State Strategic Approach: BLM-California staff will coordinate with partners to raise public awareness of the National Conservation Lands. Increased internal and external communication will enhance awareness and identity of the National Conservation Lands. A website will be developed and social media utilized to inform and educate the public about the values of the National Conservation Lands.

Goal 3A: Launch a wide-ranging public awareness initiative about the BLM's National Conservation Lands, including national and local outreach, communications, and media plans.

State Level Actions:

1. Increase use of the internet and media technologies to highlight recreation opportunities on National Conservation Lands. ▪

   a. Develop a video podcast series and Facebook pages for interpreting the National Conservation Lands for the public.

   b. Collaborate with Google Maps, Apple Maps, and Mapquest to ensure National Monuments, National Conservation Areas, and other National Conservation Land units are depicted on public online maps.

   c. Link National Conservation Lands maps interpretive and outreach materials to web-based outlets, including Quick Response (QR) codes and the Uniform Resource Locator (URL).

   d. Develop web-based interactive games to make learning about National Conservation Lands fun and engaging to the public.

2. Implement National Conservation Lands branding, logo, design criteria, consistent messaging, publication standards and web-based information established by the BLM-Washington Office. ▪

3. Expand the use of Newsbytes, BLM Daily and DOI newsletter to reach with information about the public National Conservation Lands events and programs.

   a. Employ young people through cooperative agreements with youth organizations to maintain websites and social media.

4. Improve opportunities for young adults' involvement in the management of the National Conservation Lands through partnerships, programs, and employment. ▪

   a. Develop a cooperative partnership with the National Park Service and U.S. Forest Service to engage underserved and economically disadvantaged young people from urban and rural communities.

   b. Recruit and employ bilingual BLM-California staff and offer Spanish language training. Develop programs and outreach materials for new visitors to the National Conservation Lands including Hmong, Chinese, Vietnamese, Korean, Russian, and other ethnic groups.

   c. Develop environmental education and other outreach programs to increase public awareness and knowledge about the National Conservation Lands with focus on urban populations.

5. Sponsor and support annual events such as National Trails Day, National Public Lands Day, California State Fair, Los Angeles County Fair, California Trails and Greenways Conference, and other public events. ▪

   a. Produce an annual National Conservation Lands calendar and other publication materials.

6. Incorporate science research taking place on National Conservation Lands into interpretation and outreach programs.

Goal 3B: Advance and strengthen partnerships to share stewardship and to advance the relevance of the National Conservation Lands to place-based and interest-based communities.

State Level Actions:

1. Engage Resource Advisory Councils to foster and enhance communication of the values and benefits of National Conservation Lands to local communities. ▪

2. Identify environmental education and other learning opportunities on National Conservation Lands.

   a. Design Junior Explorer programs and opportunities on National Conservation Lands.

   b. Increase the number of Take It Outside and Hands on the Land programs on National Conservation Lands.

Outdoor Summit for Youth
Expanding Horizons

In September 2012, BLM-California sponsored two Outdoor Summits for Youth in Riverside and Sacramento to convene a diverse coalition of youth organizations and partners to have a public conversation on ways to increase outreach, education, and career opportunities to low-income, economically disadvantaged young people from underserved communities throughout California. Leaders of youth organizations and representatives from other land management agencies joined BLM-California staff to discuss creating and expanding partnerships to educate, engage, and employ young people in America's Great Outdoors and the field of natural resource management. A highlight of each Summit was a panel of young people who shared their personal experiences working for government agencies, non-governmental organizations, and other organizations in natural resource management. An important outcome from the Summits was an action plan to increase opportunities for young people on public lands.

Piedras Blancas Light Station
Outstanding Natural Area

3. Develop and expand stewardship partnerships. ▪

   a. Analyze and use information gathered at 2012 Youth Summits to develop and expand youth-based partnerships.

   b. Explore expanded use of site stewards and hosts at National Conservation Lands units.

   c. Work with the Conservation Lands Foundation to launch a collaborative restoration program on National Conservation Lands.

4. Increase partnerships with writers, film makers, publishers, and artists using many media for developing materials about the National Conservation Lands.

   a. Develop opportunities for an artists-in-residence program in partnership with Friends Groups and other partners.

   b. Develop natural history guidebooks about the National Conservation Lands.

   c. Request assistance from the Conservation Lands Foundation and other partners to write articles for newspapers, magazines, and other publications.

   d. Participate in community film festivals, photo contests, and other media programs to introduce the public to the National Conservation Lands.

Goal 3C: Expand opportunities for volunteers within the National Conservation Lands.

State Level Actions:

1. Designate a National Conservation Lands volunteer coordinator for each field office. ▪

2. Collaborate with other agencies and partners to share use of scarce resources, functions, and skills to strengthen the BLM-California volunteer program.

3. Highlight volunteers, volunteer accomplishments, and opportunities in media and web pages such as Volunteer.gov.

   a. Establish a BLM-California statewide award to recognize volunteers.

   b. Host an annual event to recognize volunteers and BLM-California volunteer coordinators.

4. Sponsor at least one annual National Public Lands Day event in each field office.

5. Partner with the California Archaeological Site Stewardship Program to increase monitoring of archaeological sites on National Conservation Lands.

6. Expand volunteer opportunities for stewardship projects on National Conservation Lands.

Goal 3D: Engage the public in stewardship of the National Conservation Lands through education and interpretation.

State Level Actions:

1. Support and expand partnerships with Friends Groups, non-governmental organizations, volunteers, and other groups that assist with the management of the National Conservation Lands. ▪

   a. Expand partnerships with California Gateway Community Groups, the Conservation Lands Foundation, the Friends of the Desert Mountains, and other Friends Groups and organizations.

   b. Collaborate with other government agencies and organizations to share costs for development of environmental education programs for young people from economically disadvantaged communities. (e.g., CREEC-California Regional Environmental Education Community).

   c. Utilize the California Environmental Education Initiative curriculum developed by the California Environmental Protection Agency for school programs held on National Conservation Lands.

   d. Develop and expand place-based curricula on National Conservation Lands.

2. Expand Tread Lightly! and Leave No Trace environmental ethics training programs. ▪

3. Promote the unique values of the National Conservation Lands at gateway community visitor centers or other facilities that provide information and services to the public. ▪

4. Strengthen partnerships with gateway communities by development of cooperative agreements to expand outreach and education programs for the public.

Friends of the Desert Mountains
Santa Rosa and San Jacinto Mountains National Monument

The Friends of the Desert Mountains is a dynamic non-governmental organization that supports education, conservation, and research in the Santa Rosa and San Jacinto Mountains National Monument. In 2012, the Friends coordinated most of the volunteer programs in the Monument, totaling some 8,400 hours valued at about $183,000. The Friends have also been very successful in preserving and acquiring open space in the Coachella Valley and the surrounding desert mountains. The BLM sets broad parameters that empower the Friends organization to make decisions regarding conservation and education programs that benefit the community and visitors to the National Conservation Lands. This direct involvement promotes enthusiasm for programs that benefit the National Monument and meet the Friends' mission.

BLM-California
Volunteers

BLM is very fortunate to have the "hands on" support of hundreds of volunteers who contribute their time and hard work to helping BLM protect, preserve, and restore the National Conservation Lands in California. Last year, volunteers contributed over 36,000 hours of service towards the National Conservation Lands in California at a value of $360,000. Hosted workers paid by other organizations contributed another 27,000 hours.

Fort Ord National Monument

a. Expand development of Junior Explorer booklets. Use the interagency model developed by BLM-Oregon in partnership with the U.S. Forest Service and Fish and Wildlife Service (e.g. Wildflowers in Klamath & Lake Counties booklet).

b. Improve "trip planning" for visitors to National Conservation Lands through web-based links to maps and other outreach materials on BLM websites.

c. Expand use of social media such as Facebook, Twitter, and YouTube to share information with visitors about the National Conservation Lands.

5. Partner with other government agencies, educational institutions, and non-profit organizations to develop podcasts, video clips, and Public Service Announcements about the National Conservation Lands.

a. Create Public Service Announcements to raise public awareness of the National Conservation Lands in partnership with The Advertising Council, commonly known as the Ad Council (e.g. U.S. Forest Service Smokey Bear fire prevention ads).

b. Utilize Arcata Field Office Outdoors Cool Public Service Announcements as a model to raise public awareness of the National Conservation Lands.

Goal 3E: Recruit, train, and mentor young people so that they may engage professionally in recreation, education, and stewardship on National Conservation Lands.

State Level Actions:

1. Recruit and retain young people from diverse backgrounds to fill seasonal and permanent employment positions with BLM-California. ▪

2. Recruit veterans for academic internships and to fill seasonal and permanent employment positions with BLM-California.

3. Provide internet and social media links focused on young people discovering and learning about the values of the National Conservation Lands. ▪

4. Provide internships and employment opportunities through youth organizations, academic institutions, and non-governmental organizations on National Conservation Lands units. ▪

5. Identify and communicate opportunities for young people to become involved in science and research priorities and projects on National Conservation Lands. ■

   a. Develop and expand cooperative agreements with colleges and universities for student research projects with an emphasis on National Conservation Lands.

   b. Recruit undergraduate and graduate students for academic internships on National Conservation Lands.

   c. Develop place-based curricula for use in primary and secondary schools linked to specific values and features of National Conservation Lands.

6. Establish a field school offering college credit courses that engage economically disadvantaged young adults from underserved communities.

Nick's Interns

King Range National Conservation Area

Nick's Interns was founded by a local family on the North Coast in memory of their son who worked as a student intern at the King Range National Conservation Area. The program, funded through a private endowment and donations, offers paid internships for young adults to advance efforts to break the cycle of poverty and drug abuse that afflict youth in many rural communities. Internships for students give them skills to become involved in community efforts to restore watersheds and assist with other conservation projects on public lands. The students gain confidence and work skills and learn about natural resource management careers with the BLM and other government agencies. Graduates of the program have gone on to pursue successful careers in natural resource management and other professions.

Pacific Crest National Scenic Trail

Theme 4: Optimizing the BLM Commitment to Conservation

Strategic Approach: BLM-California will communicate the values and management of the National Conservation Lands at workshops, meetings, and events as well as through social media. The five-year strategy will be implemented statewide to ensure consistent management of the National Conservation Lands.

Goal 4A: Improve internal communication and understanding of the National Conservation Lands and its potential to enhance the BLM as a whole.

State Level Actions:

1. Develop key messages that express the unique role and opportunities of the National Conservation Lands.

2. Provide training for BLM-California State, District, and Field Office staff with planning and design of interpretive materials.

    a. Encourage BLM-California staff to complete certifications from the National Association for Interpretation.

    b. Develop a cadre of BLM-California interpretive specialists to provide on-site training for friends groups, partners, and volunteers.

3. Archive and store multi-media products about the National Conservation Lands on a SharePoint site.

4. Schedule quarterly conference calls with BLM-California program managers and other staff to communicate and share information about the National Conservation Lands.

5. Share knowledge and expertise among staff about the methods used to achieve successful accomplishments in National Conservation Lands public outreach and resolution of management issues.

6. Provide copies of the *California National Conservations Lands Five Year Strategy* (2013–2018) document with State Directors and Program Leads in other states.

Goal 4B: Cultivate shared responsibility for the National Conservation Lands conservation mandate as an integral part of BLM's multiple-use, sustained-yield mission.

State Level Actions:

1. Cooperate with partners and provide assistance with the administration of cooperative agreements, contracts, and volunteer management.

    a. Initiate a training program with the Conservation Lands Foundation, Friends Groups, and other stakeholders about the BLM procedures and guidelines for administration and management of cooperative agreements.

    b. Schedule an annual meeting between BLM-California staff and the Conservation Lands Foundation, Friends Groups, stakeholders, and volunteers to discuss the National Conservation Lands issues.

2. Conduct a biennial National Conservation Lands and Recreation workshop with BLM-California staff and encourage participation of Friends Groups, non-governmental organizations, stakeholders, and other partners.

3. Ensure that National Conservation Lands program managers participate in other statewide meetings or workshops to ensure integration with other BLM-California programs such as public affairs, fire, engineering, cadastral survey, law enforcement, etc.

4. Coordinate Land and Water Conservation Fund packages (both core and collaborative) internally and with other agencies well in advance of proposal deadlines.

5. Identify grants and fundraising opportunities that could be initiated with the Conservation Lands Foundation to help finance research, education, and other programs to benefit the National Conservation Lands.

Goal 4C: Clearly understand, define, and support staffing needs, and administratively organize the National Conservation Lands areas to operate as a cross-cutting program within the BLM.

State Level Actions:

1. Build skills of BLM-California staff and community partners to coordinate partnerships, write grant proposals, and train and supervise volunteers.

The Student Conservation Association, National Conservation Lands
Youth Corps Team

The Student Conservation Association, through an innovative partnership with BLM, is working to reconnect America's young people with the outdoors while benefitting the National Conservation Lands. The National Conservation Lands Youth Corps Teams make a significant six to nine month volunteer commitment to complete on-the-ground conservation projects such as trail construction and maintenance, restoration activities, invasive weed eradication, wilderness resource monitoring, and environmental education. During the last three years alone, the Youth Corps Teams have completed more than 200 miles of trail maintenance; 200 acres of restoration activities; installed 20 miles of fence to protect wilderness values; closed 40 miles of unauthorized motorized vehicle routes; and developed 35 environmental education programs for visitors. In addition, the Youth Corps Teams play an essential role in connecting young people to their public lands and instilling in them a sense of stewardship.

Wall Canyon Wilderness Study Area

2. Assess current staffing levels and future skills needed for optimum management of the National Conservation Lands units to meet BLM national and California objectives.

3. Position BLM programmatic staff to share resources and staff expertise across the state to implement National Conservation Lands priorities.

Goal 4D: Ensure that the National Conservation Lands budget coordinates with other BLM programs. Set clear expectations and procedures for cross-programmatic budget development, priority setting, and reporting of accomplishments.

State Level Actions

1. Ensure that each Monument and National Conservation Area has a unique organization code in the Federal Budget Management System (FBMS) and that these codes are used to identify workload accomplishments. ▪

2. Develop an implementation strategy for management actions identified in land use plans that contain National Conservation Lands units and identify workload priorities at the State and District level. ▪

3. Provide input to the BLM-Washington Office with performance measures for each component of the National Conservation Lands.

4. Participate in a national effort to identify priority program elements for Monuments and NCAs.

5. Aggressively pursue innovative and alternative funding for the National Conservation Lands through such programs as challenge cost share, science research, and recreation fee collection.

6. Meet frequently with interdisciplinary program managers during the development of the annual National Conservation Lands budget to advocate for and ensure consistent funding for the program.

7. Encourage managers of National Conservation Lands units develop management plans that are tiered to the state and national goals for the National Conservation Lands.

50th Anniversary of the Wilderness Act

The 50th Anniversary of the landmark 1964 Wilderness Act is September 3, 2014. This historic event will provide an opportunity for the public to learn about wilderness, participate in the shared legacy of wilderness stewardship, and better understand the importance of these special places in sustaining the health and diversity of our public lands. The BLM, along with U.S. Forest Service, National Park Service, Fish and Wildlife Service, wilderness advocacy groups, environmental organizations, academic institutions, Native Americans, and other groups are planning activities, events, and service projects throughout the year. A National Wilderness Conference scheduled for October 15–19, 2014 in Albuquerque, NM will be the culmination of the yearlong celebration and highlight how wilderness contributes to our nation's health and well-being. The conference will be a four-day event including presentations, panels, displays, and field trips, best practices, social gatherings, and sharing information and emerging issues in wilderness.

Trinity Wild and Scenic River
BLM/CA/GI-2013-004+610